SMALL FURRY ANIMALS

Squirrel

SMALL FURRY ANIMALS

Squirrel

Ting Morris

Illustrated by Graham Rosewarne

A⁺

Smart Apple Media

It's a cold, frosty morning, and the park is covered by a blanket of snow. You can see a trail of footprints leading to a big tree. And you find empty nutshells scattered all around.

4

Who could have made the tracks
and cracked those nuts?

Turn the page and take a closer look.

5

A squirrel left the tracks in the snow. Can you see her, up in the tree? She's rushing home to her warm nest, where she spends most of the winter. Today she came down early to dig up some nuts she buried last fall. She had no trouble finding them, even though they were hidden under a thick layer of snow.

Gray squirrels

Gray squirrels belong to a group of animals called rodents, which means "gnawing." This is because they have strong front teeth, which they use to gnaw nuts, pinecones, and bark. Gray squirrels are from North America and were taken to Europe as well more than 120 years ago.

A warm winter home

Squirrels make a warm, waterproof nest for the winter. This is called a drey. Dreys are built on a sturdy branch close to the trunk of a tall tree. A squirrel wedges bundles of sticks and twigs into the branch fork and weaves them into a round nest. To make it hollow, the builder gets in and turns around and around. Inside, the drey is lined with bark, moss, grass, feathers, or other soft materials.

WHAT ARE MAMMALS?

All rodents, including squirrels, are mammals. A mammal has hair or fur on its body to help keep it warm. Baby mammals are fed with milk from their mother's body. Human beings are mammals, too.

After breakfast, the squirrel is ready for another snooze. It has started snowing again, and an icy wind is whistling through the branches. The squirrel wraps herself up in her tail, but she can still feel the cold. It was much cozier when she shared her winter home with two other squirrels. But now her nest mates have moved out, and there's just one bushy tail to snuggle under.

Home to home

Squirrels usually have two or three homes and move from one to the other every few days. If a nest is damaged in a storm or attacked by an enemy, the squirrels spend the night in one of their other homes.

Red cousins

The red squirrel is smaller than the gray. It spends a lot of time in the treetops of pine forests. It has bright, chestnut-colored fur, ear tufts, and a long, bushy tail. In North America, red squirrels are found in evergreen forests from Alaska to South Carolina.

NEST CONVERSION

Instead of building a drey, squirrels sometimes move into a hollow tree. They might fix up a woodpecker's former nest hole with a few twigs and leaves. Winter dens are lined with moss for extra warmth.

Summer home

In the summer, squirrels build flimsy nests where they can take a quick rest. These summer homes are just a shallow platform of twigs. An old bird's nest can be a handy starting point for the builder.

9

Spring has arrived at last! It's warm and sunny, and lots of squirrels are scouring the park for food. How many grays can you spot? There's plenty to eat now: leaves, buds, bulbs, shoots, and roots, as well as last year's stock of buried nuts. Our gray squirrel is enjoying a sweet, sappy treat. With her sharp teeth, she gnaws the bark of a tree and then peels it off to get at the juicy sap below.

Long leapers

Squirrels have short front legs and long, powerful hind legs for leaping. They can jump more than 20 feet (6 m)! Their bushy tail, which is almost as long as their body, is used for balance when leaping and climbing, for signaling to friends and enemies, as a blanket in the winter, and as a sunshade in the summer. The gray squirrel weighs about one pound (500 g)—nearly twice as much as a red squirrel.

Sharp claws

With their strong feet and sharp claws, squirrels can scamper up tree trunks and scale brick walls. They can also hang upside down and flat against a tree trunk to pick nuts. Their front feet have four clawed toes, and their hind feet have five.

front foot

hind foot

Nutcrackers

A squirrel's teeth work like a pair of nutcrackers. It has four big incisors at the front that grow all the time. To keep them short and sharp, a squirrel has to gnaw hard food every day. Don't ever annoy a squirrel—it can give you a nasty bite!

"Chuck-chuck-chuck chiree-chirrrrr!" The gray squirrel hears the males' noisy chatter, but at first she goes on eating. Who will she choose to be her mate? Three suitors have come to chase her. One is flicking his tail and slapping the bark with his front paws to try to get noticed.

Look, now she's dashing up the tree, and the males are rushing after her. They leap through the branches, then race up, down, and around the trunk before speeding across the grass.

Courtship

Female squirrels mate with males in order to produce babies. Courtship includes noisy chattering, tail flicking, and chasing. Several male rivals usually compete for a female. The first male to arrive starts the chase, and this can last all day until the female signals her decision. She chatters softly, making a low "tuk-tuk" noise and allowing the winner to come close to her. The tired rivals leave without a fight.

Different species

Red and gray squirrels have similar habits, but they don't mix. Members of the two different species sometimes get into fights. If they live in the same woods, they might borrow each other's drey, but they never occupy it at the same time.

A SAFE HOME

Gray squirrels are pregnant for about six weeks. During that time, they build a safe nest for their babies. This litter drey must be well-hidden in a hollow tree or high up in the branches. The mother-to-be builds a sturdy framework of twigs and lines it with grass.

13

The mother squirrel is watching over her babies. They were born two days ago and are still blind and helpless. She can't leave her young for long, because they need her milk to grow. She knows she needs to eat to stay healthy, but for now she makes do with nuts she stored near the nest. She's on guard duty day and night, and if another squirrel comes too close, she chases it away.

Cry-babies

A mother suckles her young for 8 to 10 weeks. She has eight nipples, so all the babies can suck milk at the same time. Young squirrels squeal loudly for their mother, and she always answers their cries.

ONE-PARENT FAMILY

Female squirrels have one litter a year, or two if there is plenty of food in the area. The first litter is born between February and April, and the second is born in the summer. Squirrels can have up to six young, but usually there are no more than four babies in a litter.

Teething

When they are about four weeks old, the little squirrels open their eyes for the first time and start teething. As soon as their teeth begin to grow, the baby squirrels chew bark and twigs inside the nest to sharpen them. When the youngsters are about 10 weeks old, they leave the nest.

15

"Tu-whit tu-whoo!" When the mother squirrel hears an owl hooting, she knows there could be danger nearby. She must move her young to a safer place. She knows other dreys in the park, but she can take only one baby squirrel at a time. She picks them up carefully with her mouth. Moving quickly through the dark, she carries her young one by one to a hollow tree close by.

Furry

At about three weeks of age, baby squirrels are fully furred. Their first coat is soft and fluffy, and young gray squirrels have red fur patches. A squirrel grows adult gray fur when it is fully independent, at around three months of age.

LOSING INTEREST

Once the young squirrels can eat solid food, their mother stops feeding them milk. She goes back to her old dreys and visits the youngsters now and then until they have left home. Then she leaves them on their own.

Pass the flea

Squirrels carry a lot of fleas in their fur, as well as mites and lice. At about seven weeks of age, a young squirrel has a fine coat of hair, which becomes infested with its mother's fleas. The fleas stay and travel with the squirrels, but squirrels don't seem to be bothered by them.

What's on the menu?

The gray squirrel feeds on nuts, seeds, bark, buds, fruit, fungi, and insects. Even birds' eggs and nestlings are on the menu. It is an expert at picking pinecones and nuts high up in the branches, and uses the same method for reaching hanging baskets of food put out for birds. It dangles from a twig (or a wire) by its hind feet and reaches for the food with its front paws. Squirrels get most of the water they need from the food they eat.

It's playtime around the new nest. Exploring is fun, but cracking nuts is not as easy as it looks. Luckily their mother is a patient teacher, and they copy everything she does. One curious youngster always gets into trouble and then screams for help. He's learned another lesson today—don't tease birds!

FINDING FOOD

Squirrels use their eyes and nose to find food. They press their nose to the ground to sniff out hidden supplies of food, called caches. Since they can't smell the difference between their own and other squirrels' buried nuts, they often dig up a neighbor's cache.

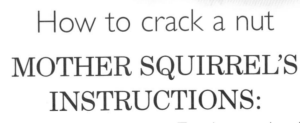

How to crack a nut

MOTHER SQUIRREL'S INSTRUCTIONS:

Hold the nut between your paws. Turn it around and weigh it (light nuts don't have a good seed). Bite a hole in the top of the nut, then pry the two halves of the shell apart with your front teeth. Take out the nut and eat it.

The young squirrels have left their nest and are now out on their own. They don't see their mother any more, and older squirrels often chase them away. There are lots of dangers, since many other animals are on the prowl. Using an older squirrel's drey is risky, too. Just when a youngster settles down, it gets noticed and is chased out. One young squirrel tries building his own drey with grass, but he soon finds he's heavier than he thought!

20

Enemies and dangers

Squirrels can sometimes live to the age of 12. But most die in the first few months after leaving the litter drey. Their enemies include hawks, owls, cats, foxes, weasels, and snakes. Many are also killed by cars and fires.

weasel

owl

snake

hawk

fox

cat

Squirrels need to be quick and alert.

Face-wiping

Squirrels mark the route they regularly take by wiping their face on branches. This leaves a smelly fluid from their mouth, and each squirrel has its own personal smell.

21

an you see the three young squirrels? They are fully grown now and look just like the older squirrels that used to chase them away. Now they do the scolding if new neighbors bother them. It's fall, and the whole day is spent collecting, eating, and storing food. This will be the youngsters' first winter, and they know there's lots of work to do. They carry nuts to a good hiding place. Then they dig a hole with their front paws, put the nuts in, scrape the soil and grass back into place, and press the mound down. The ground is turning into a larder.

Busy days

Squirrels work during the day and sleep at night. Their busiest time is in late summer and fall, when they bury food for the winter. At the same time, they have to eat a lot to put on extra fat. So they are out from dawn until dusk without even stopping for a nap.

WHERE HAVE ALL THE REDS GONE?

Some people think that gray squirrels have chased away red squirrels, but this is not really true. Reds find most of their food in the treetops. As more and more conifers are felled, their food disappears and they starve or move away.

Squirrel chat

Squirrels make scolding and chattering sounds. Listen for their noisy chirps, grunts, and squeals. Red squirrels make higher, more piercing sounds than their gray cousins.

23

The young squirrel has changed into his warm winter coat and is fat and furry now. All he needs to get through the cold months is a nice warm drey. In his search for a good place, he's found this tree hole. Have you seen it before? The squirrel probably doesn't remember coming here when he was a baby, but he likes the looks of it. He'll be snug in here and even warmer when other squirrels come for the winter. Perhaps his brother and sister will join him in his new, cozy den!

Black and white

Gray squirrels can have unusual coloring. Some are all black. If you ever see a white squirrel, it's not a ghost but an albino. An albino is an animal that lacks the usual color and has red eyes.

WINTER COAT

In the fall, squirrels molt into a winter coat. Gray squirrels replace their thin, yellowish-brown fur with a thicker, silvery winter coat. Their tail gets bushier, and their feet become thickly covered with fur. The molting process takes up to six weeks.

25

Females give birth to a litter in the spring.

SQUIRREL CIRCLE OF LIFE

Squirrels go on mating chases late in the winter. Females then build litter dreys.

Squirrels are fully grown when they are about a year old.

Young squirrels
leave their nest in
the summer.

In the fall, squirrels fatten
up and store nuts and
seeds for the winter.

Squirrels move
into winter
dreys in
November.

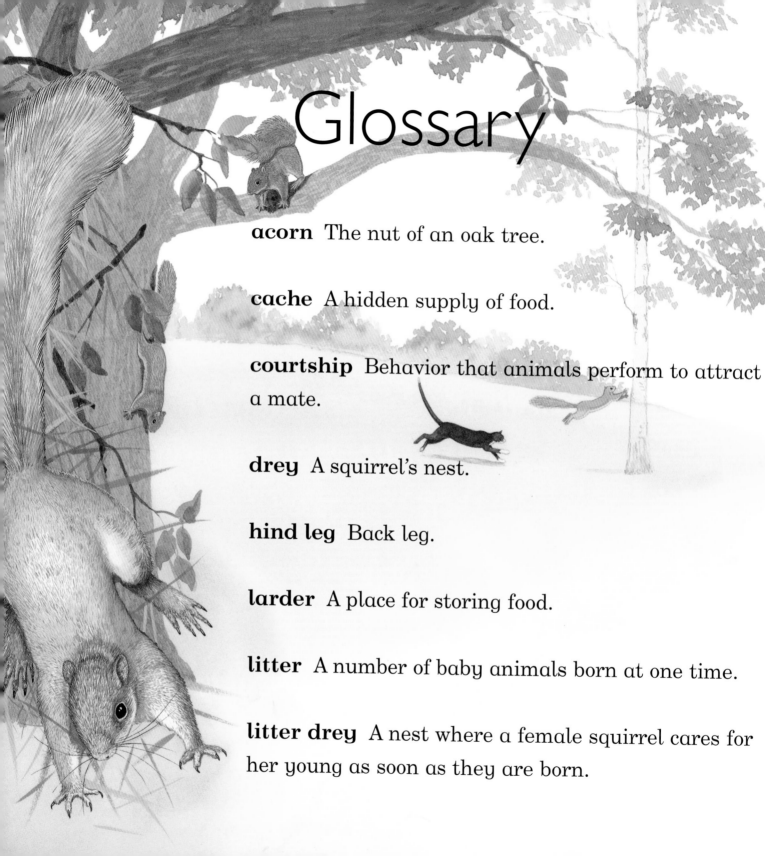

Glossary

acorn The nut of an oak tree.

cache A hidden supply of food.

courtship Behavior that animals perform to attract a mate.

drey A squirrel's nest.

hind leg Back leg.

larder A place for storing food.

litter A number of baby animals born at one time.

litter drey A nest where a female squirrel cares for her young as soon as they are born.

mate When a male and female animal come together to make babies.

molt To shed hair and make room for new fur growth.

nestling A baby bird in the nest.

rodent A small mammal that gnaws food with its strong front teeth.

sap The juice inside a plant that serves as its food.

suckle To feed milk to a young animal.

teethe To grow teeth.

INDEX

Published by Smart Apple Media
2140 Howard Drive West, North Mankato, Minnesota 56003

Designed by Helen James
Illustrated by Graham Rosewarne

Photographs by Corbis (Niall Benvie, Gary W. Carter, Roger
Wilmshurst; Frank Lane Picture Agency, Raymond Gehman, Darrell
Gulin, George McCarthy, Roy Morsch, Jamie Harron; Papilio)

Printed and bound in Thailand

Library of Congress Cataloging-in-Publication Data

Morris, Ting.
Squirrel / by Ting Morris.
p. cm. — (Small furry animals)
ISBN 1-58340-520-8
1. Squirrels—Juvenile literature. [1. Squirrels.] I. Title. II. Small furry
animals (Mankato, Minn.)

QL737.R68M67 2004
599.36—dc22   2003067255

First Edition

9 8 7 6 5 4 3 2 1